Colorful
Days

FIRST EDITION

Series Editor Deborah Lock; **Senior Art Editor** Tory Gordon-Harris; **Design Assistant** Sadie Thomas;
Production Claire Pearson; **DTP Designer** Almudena Díaz; **Jacket Designer** Peter Radcliffe;
Reading Consultant Cliff Moon, M.Ed.

THIS EDITION

Editorial Management by Oriel Square
Produced for DK by WonderLab Group LLC
Jennifer Emmett, Erica Green, Kate Hale, *Founders*

Editors Grace Hill Smith, Libby Romero, Michaela Weglinski;
Photography Editors Kelley Miller, Annette Kiesow, Nicole DiMella;
Managing Editor Rachel Houghton; **Designers** Project Design Company;
Researcher Michelle Harris; **Copy Editor** Lori Merritt; **Indexer** Connie Binder; **Proofreader** Larry Shea;
Reading Specialist Dr. Jennifer Albro; **Curriculum Specialist** Elaine Larson

Published in the United States by DK Publishing
1745 Broadway, 20th Floor, New York, NY 10019
Copyright © 2023 Dorling Kindersley Limited
DK, a Division of Penguin Random House LLC
22 23 24 25 26 10 9 8 7 6 5 4 3 2 1
001-333470-May/2023

A catalog record for this book
is available from the Library of Congress.
HC ISBN: 978-0-7440-6849-8
PB ISBN: 978-0-7440-6850-4

DK books are available at special discounts when purchased in bulk for sales promotions, premiums,
fundraising, or educational use. For details, contact: DK Publishing Special Markets,
1745 Broadway, 20th Floor, New York, NY 10019
SpecialSales@dk.com

Printed and bound in China

The publisher would like to thank the following for their kind permission to reproduce their images:
a=above; c=center; b=below; l=left; r=right; t=top; b/g=background

Shutterstock.com: Africa Studio 25t, Gunnerchu 4bc, Happy Hirtzel 26-27, Songdech Kothmongkol 11c

Cover images: *Front:* **Dreamstime.com:** Allegro7 cla, crb, Benchart, Raman Maisei cra;
Back: **Shutterstock.com:** Fantastic Day cla, robuart cra

All other images © Dorling Kindersley
For more information see: www.dkimages.com

For the curious
www.dk.com

Colorful Days

Elizabeth Hester

Come and
play with me.

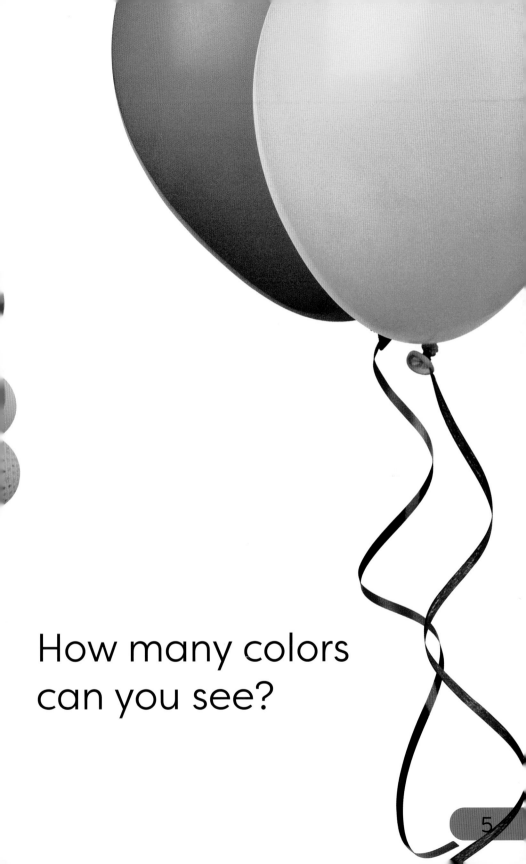

How many colors
can you see?

white

We can play
in the cold,
white snow.

We can look at
the purple flowers.

purple

We can run
around the trees
that have
pink blossoms.

 pink

gray

We can play
with the small,
gray rabbits.

We can look
at the boats
on the blue sea.

 **blue**

We can play
near the
tall, yellow
sunflowers.

yellow

orange

We can eat
a frozen orange
treat.

 **red**

We can kick
the red leaves.
We can also pick
the red apples.

black

We can look
at the black ants.
We can see the
black beetle.

We can croak
like the small,
brown frogs.

 **brown**

We can walk by
the tall, green trees.

green

We can hang up
silver balls and
put on gold crowns.

silver and gold

silver

gold

How many colors
can you see?

Glossary

blue
the color of some toy cars, blueberries, and the sea

green
the color of pine trees, tree frogs, and some parrots

orange
the color of pumpkins, carrots, and oranges

red
the color of some leaves, apples, and holly berries

yellow
the color of bananas, lemons, and sunflowers

Quiz

Answer the questions to see what you have learned. Check your answers with an adult.

What color is each of these things?

1. Some blossoms on trees in the spring
2. Some small, fuzzy rabbits
3. Some ants and beetles
4. Small frogs that blend in with leaves
5. A crown

1. Pink 2. Gray 3. Black 4. Brown or green 5. Gold